Other Books by Bill Kushner

Night Fishing (1980)
Head (1986)
Love Uncut (1990)
He Dreams of Waters (2000)
That April (2000)
In The Hairy Arms of Whitman (2003)
In Sunsetland With You (2007)

WALKING AFTER MIDNIGHT

Bill Kushner

SPUYTEN DUYVIL

New York City

ISBN 978-1-933132-91-4

Cover and drawings by Pamela Lawton

My thanks to Ruth Altmann, Don Yorty, R.A. Carlson and
Phyllis Wat for their inspiration and support.

Library of Congress Cataloging-in-Publication Data
Kushner, William.
Walking after midnight / Bill Kushner.
p. cm.
ISBN 978-1-933132-91-4
I. Title.
PS3561.U78W35 2011
811'.54--dc22
2011023767

for Lewis Warsh

WALKING AFTER MIDNIGHT

WHEN I WAS FIVE

What I was was tiny balls of tinsel and
lust. When I was five I was already
in deepest love. You can say what you
want, and you will, but back then that
love it was love. I would croon to my
pillow, love oh love. I would suck on
my bottle of Yoo-Hoo, love oh love.
I would watch my father paint a room,
love oh love, and he would say Shut up.
I would watch my mother cook and broom,
oh love Mom love, and she would say Shut
up. All for love when love then was now
that was love. My restless bed awake
with it, love. Would gather sticks of wood
from the forest of love. Would I frighten
the wolves? yes, for love was love, and there
was none other. Would I even terrify the
sparrows and the doves? yes, for love was yes
love. I ate wild berries and ripe cherries, and
with my mouth as red as new blood, I sang it:
love love love. I grew angry when I could not
see my love, could not smell my love, oh love.
Everyone else I knew grew out of it, gathered
their stars and drove off in their shiny new cars,
but not I, for somehow, year after year, there I
was, still five, and they don't allow me to drive,
no not I and my heart, drugged on love. Dear
heart, you still drugged on love? And my poor
heart's answer? Yes, love, yes you and all you,
love, love, laave.

MARILYN MONROE

There are certain things that seem to
truly exist. I live in a room with 4
walls. In stairs in walls in peeling
paint, I float within. This pen in
my hand from who knows where or
what ghost holds it who writes these
words. I caress the tooth of my tiger
cat, Blinky. And there lie the teeth of
my other cats, Smokey, Bandit and Pee
Wee. "God loves you," I often whisper
to them, "and so do I." Sometimes,
when I say my prayers at night, I like
to add, "and God bless Dick Nixon," as
I spit 3 times and cross myself twice. I
sleep with a rag doll I like to call Lenin,
in honor of my parents who came all the
way from Russia, just imagine that journey
through thick and thin. Like many young
boys, I was fascinated by dinosaurs. I
would play in my room for hours with my
plastic dinosaurs and a picture of Marilyn
Monroe I took off a calendar, I forget what
year. I'd pretend that the bad dinosaurs
were attacking poor poor Marilyn, "oh dear,"
she'd say, poor thing. Most nights, they
ate her and ate her until there was nothing
too much left, oh a tooth of hers, or two.
But some nights, I'd come and rescue her
from those terrible rapacious beasts, and then
I'd keep her safe from them, forever and
ever. She'd sleep with me, under my pillow,
sweet Miss Marilyn Monroe, safe, safe from
all harm.

WILD DESIRES

From the very moment Kitty looked into the
stranger's steely eyes, she knew, Kitty knew.
She'd begun to wonder what a girl like her was
doing in this wild country, but now she knew.
Watching him from behind the trunk of a tree
in this wild forest of wild desires, Kitty knew,
as he fished the tides with his hard taut lines,
she learned that her passion was as untamed
as the man she loved. "Ma'am, but you can
sure cook up a fish," he grinned, as she just
devoured him with her eyes, but oh where in
the devil were her trembling hands? "It's
this heat," she told him, as he looked up from
the plate to see her, so flushed, staring at him,
and in an instant, he knew, and her secret was
lost! This damn man, he was just as wild as
the West itself, and with one quick move, why
there he was, down on his knees between her
legs and the legs of the kitchen table, and there
was only the heat of his deep probing tongue
between them, and his fiery mouth of salt and
bones, and swallowing her, her helpless to even
scream, down and down, and down and down!

CHINA

Mother digs and digs in the back yard.
"What's she digging for?" Father comes
along and asks. "Beats me, Pa," I answer.
He and I, we just stare and stare at her on
her knees and digging away. She gets her
a little bit of the dirt with her little shovel,
and she tosses it onto the little pile of dirt
by her side, turns and keeps on digging.
"Hey Ma, are you digging for oil or what?
for gold?" Pa shouts out, and he sorta laughs,
nervous like, my Pa's a kinda nervous guy.
But my Ma doesn't even bother to answer,
just shakes her head and she keeps digging.
"China," Pa says. "Why, the woman, she's
off digging her way to China!" "Oh, Pa, I
don't really think so," I have to chime in.
"I know. I know," Pa agrees. "It's prob'ly
just flowers like a woman thing. Or maybe
tomatoes. Now there is a woman she knows
what to do with tomatoes, my. It's how she
landed me. Through your Daddy's tummy."
Ma keeps a digging on, and Pa and I we just
stand watching. "I still think it's China," Pa,
he finally whispers. "China, it has to be that
goddam flying China, I swear."

DOROTHY, I THINK

She had a habit of rolling her great blues upwards
Into a large suitcase, and there would be home
Only her head popped out every now and then
Her hand down the front of your pants
And even then it was necessary to look fast and
At a small Dalmation restaurant on Butter Street
Dorothy looked vaguely sad. "Oh, well" she said
Totally unhinged when "Beefy" Johnson got himself killed
By a rejected faggot boyfriend, his ex-wife
Roy sighed. "Leave town, I suppose" he said
When Margaret Gridley appeared on the scene
And always the last one to leave. She went home and went to bed
He would kill himself just to face reality
"Infantine." She got the word from Henry James who got it from God

I'M YOUR MAN

Me, I'm a man. I'm a seething being. Somehow
I believed I was sent here to this alien corn to
it was never unbearable but it was never pleasant
either. Me, I'm drinking your water and trying to
decide what line shall I next. Shall I just throw
all caution to the wind and tell you? Shall I tell you
of me the people? The people, I say, can't seem to
help their sidewalks, oh dear me. A rat along the
tracks stops still and looks at me as if I am cheese,
oh dear me, cheese. A hot truck stands shocked. A
trucker stands scratching himself and laughs, laughs.
Wait I think I'm okay I'm straight straight no gay gay.

My father, he knew, yet he loved me, couldn't, I couldn't
figure out why. Waking me, "Get up, lazy!" and up I'd get.
But it was like I had slept the sleep of the dead. Dear
Father, I see you midnights, see your ghostly strolls upon
the ramparts, saying, "Awake and sing to me again, my
son," and my arms reach out. Dear Papa, let this poem hold
you. It's like walking in a strange city and stopping to look
high up at a window in a swaying building, and remembering
a night, a long ago night, when I made true love there, yes,
sweet sweet love there, to a beautiful woman, or to a beau-
tiful man. It was there I was held tightly, all through
that night, "No, never let me go," head high, I whisper
to no one, to a damn darkened window, "Never let me go."

WALKING AFTER MIDNIGHT

Can't sleep, can't sleep. Sad trees, sad
trees, don't, don't weep. One tree full of
wavy leaves, the next tree just a skeleton,
dead, death, why? I tiptoe by. Someone's
left a cake out. 2 houses dark, sleeping side
by side, boo, I can see you two, for shame.
Deck chair for Daddy to sit in, wait, wait,
but for what, what? Me, I haven't spoken to
him, my Dad, for years now, years, so why,
why of a sudden do I wonder on him now?
Heck, I just like to sit, chin in hand, as I gaze
amazed at the naked scenery. Hello you
moon, there's a light comes on, are you me?
but soft, there's a car comes ever so softly,
now where you been? One turn of the road
and gone, you're gone. Hello, little hillock,
and what will I do with you but climb, yearn,
climb? God, I need a bath a bed and beyond.
Your address says 2612, and where then
shall we be? If a tree could speak, what
would a tree speak? Let me but lean against
you, tree, nice tree, are these my hairy arms or
yours? Oh speak to me, speak to me, because
I'll listen, oh baby baby, to whatever you say.

BUT

it's still not me, I don't see the moon. Have
the pirates come for you, moon, and are you
drowning in the ocean, and must I swim out
and save you? I stood and stood outside your
house, but that was just love was just staring
and staring, as you moved within it, in, out, in.
I stand where the damn storm knocked down the
dead tree, that's me, I stand on the dead tree
and listen to it sighing, ah poor me. Inside, but
why are you staring? and whatever are you
thinking, are you thinking of me? Poetry is a
crazy but that was a long time ago and some
other poor sailor with his shipwrecks and some
other moon oh there you've stopped, breathless
at last, and now let me touch you, you staring out.
There's the little plant I brought you beside you
in a purple bloom, but what is that blue thing?
well blue is blue, as I watch you dreamily disrobe,
eyes wide-eyed as 2 unread books. Love, love, I
wandered through fireflies to find you, love was all
for you, and soon you'll turn and you'll turn out
the light and still no moon, are you drowned, moon,
as my dead tree keeps sobbing why oh why, why me?

GHOSTS

A lot of people, a lot of extremely nutty people
see ghosts and they scream or don't scream, it's
all the same to me. Hello, this is the ghost of me
talking to the ghost of you. Me, I was but a dream
ketchup sandwiches I ate under deep deep
cover, when then was whatever, need I tell you
more? You get a little nervous when two eyes
from the past beam on you, as if chances were
men, and I mean, real men. Back then, I did a
lot of things, dumb things, a lot of things. Oh sure
I delivered your messages from the way beyond,
hey you, take that, hey you, you take that back.
You are a poet but you secretly wish you were
a rock star, so there you go head into the park
way past dark, and it's love on a swing. I mean
it just seems weird to always be this weird person
thinks words, crazy words, while the ghost of kids
screams, crazy kid dreams. I just don't think I'm
normal, so do you, huh, you? Ghost nods what looks
to be a no, and then up ghost floats, and I'm alone,
at last, alone. Alone, but the little swing, eeks, no,
keeps swinging. Don't go. Please. Please don't go.

TREE SAYS

Tree says, "This is the town, sir, that sprang
up around me. First I got scared of 'em,
for what were they doing here? with all
their candy kisses and kids and cats making
all that noise so a tree can't sleep. Me, a
tree likes his peace and quiet. To stare up
at a moon, maybe sing to it quietly, just
me, just you, we'll find a cozy spot to
cuddle and coo. A tree can fall in love, too,
you know, so you can just kiss my leaves.
Me, I've seen what goes on inside of your
houses, and sometimes it is not all that
pretty. Why, one night past midnight I saw
a man, a very young man, rush out of that dark
house I saw you, sir, just come out of so fast.
I saw the kid heading toward me in a big rush,
and he sits down beneath me, and him cursing
away. "I'll show him, that damn old bastard!"
he shouts back to his house. "Calling me that,
that name!" What name? Who's he mean? I
wonder. His father? And then the young man,
he gets up and he walks quick down that dark
street and away, and it's been years, many
years, and I haven't seen him since. Sometimes
I do wonder whatever happened to him. These
young people here they are so restless. But oh
sir, why are you weeping, why? Was the boy,
was he your son? But I didn't know! Please do
not weep. Oh why do you walk away, shaking
your head? oh please don't leave me, don't leave."

FEBRUARY

February 2, full moon. The thing of it is,
she thinks, not to think of it, the cop
undressing, the cold of his lips, his body,
his naked kiss. It's so quiet in here,
it gives me the shivers, her breathing
him in, is that furnace breathing? the mice
in the pipes, are they making love? more
Mickeys, more Minnies, ecstasy, ecstacies,
but I had to call him, I had to, I swear I
heard something down there, a prowler,
as she watches him dressing, he dresses so
carefully, carefully, then the tucking in,
the cradling, his lovechild, his gun. Would
he stick it in her, that hot black thing, be-
fore he left? "If you get down on your knees,"
he'd say, "and ask me nicely." I like these
drawings, he smiles, murmurs, nice teeth.
Kids drawings, she offers, stretching her legs.
"You like my legs?" "Oh my God, yes,"
he blushes, "but don't, don't start me again."
He'll stomp into the cold and snow, she won-
ders, and leave me without a thought. Or,
maybe one thought. Whore. Dying for it.
Is it zero yet? he shivers. The snap of the
air. Pure white of the snow. No blood on it
yet, thank God. Yeah, zero. God, zero.

THE LOVESONG OF
LEONARD & MARY

Leonard, he works night and day on their
house. He sings to it, my darling blumber
lumber. When Death comes, Leonard thinks,
I shall be here in this here chair in this old
house, a rockin' to the oldies. Sometimes,
Leonard thinks, the gods they take a human
form of the form of a human. And we shall
sing of the rapture, she sings on tiptoes and
sings. There comes a light, she sings, come
and come to bed with me, she sings and sings.
She takes him home and she dresses and she
undresses his sad wounds. We could join the
flowers, she sings, or the birds, see them love
flying up there? yes like a songbird, she sings.
Well, shiver my timbers, Leonard sings to her,
and sings and he sings.

THE LIFEGUARD SEAT

The lifeguard seat is empty.
Ssh, he is swimming, no,
floating, red Speedo, lazily.
There's just the barest hint
of a sun, floating up there, see?
Floating around and around,
so lazily, lazily.

TREES

An early bird, I live in trees, whose leaves tell me
"leave." So I leave. I climb down, and begin to
find words for cherries, words to eat. Then you
come swinging along and singing a song. Would
you like my cherry? So you do, you take my cherry
and so what? I put my lips on to your lips to watch
you eat me, sweet. Funny how I grow big and bigger
below me, let's eat. So I do, and you do, and we do.
Little by little, as leaves fall all golden and screamy,
and we stay close together, golden you, cherry me.
That I remember your face when I awake, and I re-
member your face when I sleep, and that when you
are away, why I seem to weep. Why I seem to weep.

HEAVEN

That one day, he closed his eyes, just for a
Second. When he opened them again why
He thought he was in heaven. For he was
A little boy, short pants and big-eyed, playing
By the water's edge, collecting seashells, hear
The ocean roaring, his mother's voice calling:
"Don't go too far, dear!" The caws of the
Hungry seabirds, claws lifting him up, higher
And higher, so that he was one of them, a tiny
Flapping thing, a dot on the horizon, drifting
This way now that way, and his mother far below
And screaming, "Where are you, my own little
Darling?" But gone, he was gone. "Good-
Bye, Mamma, I'm gone now! For your Little
Boy Blue, he has flown!" When he opened
His eyes again, why he had to rub them, for
Again he was home, old room, old yawn. He
Kept looking around and around, but nothing,
Nothing but a blinding silence. And it was
The very first time he'd ever heard it, silence.
He began, oh softly, to cry, knowing nothing,
Not a thing, not really. He cried and he cried.

GASP

Papa and me, we walk to the park. "Why,"
Papa asks, "must you hold on to my hand so
tight? Why, you're getting so strong!" I laugh
and, as we get to the park, I look all around.
"What's that bird?" I ask. "That's a butterfly,"
he says. "A yellow butterfly. You like?" "Is
it made of butter?" I ask, "for that's a strange
little bird," I add. "It's not a bird made out of
butter," Papa says. "It's a butterfly. It's made
out of the sky. And wishes and dreams." We
watch it flutter on to a red red flower, and we
gasp as it bends to kiss it. "Why is it kissing
that flower, Papa?" "Because it's love," he
says. "Because the butterfly is in love with
the flower." "Oh," I say. "I always wondered.
So that's love." "It's like," he says, "when
your mama and I met. And we met and she
kissed me and so I kissed her and then we
had you." "Oh," I say, "oh." We watch the
butterfly as it flutters its wings as if in a lovely
ecstasy. I look up at him and I have to think.
"I wonder, Papa. After the butterfly kisses the
flower, will the flower have little pretty little
flowers like me, I wonder?" Papa smiles and
asks, "hmm, what do you think?" "I think so,
Papa, I do. Kissing is so nice. You used to
kiss me a lot once, and I really liked it, but now
you've stopped. And I miss your kisses, Papa.
I could smell in your mouth and everything in it."
"But real men don't kiss each other after a while,"
he shrugs and answers. We see the butterfly fly
up and away. We look at the blushing flowers.

"Papa, I think I'm getting sleepy." I look up,
and I see him spread his arms out, and begin
to flutter them about. "Well," he says, "let's
us pretend we are butterflies, just you and I,
it's our secret, and let's us fly away fly away
home." And so away. We do. Away we fly home.

Today I woke up and my Dad was gone.
"Dad? Dad? Where are you?" I called
out. But there was no one, after all my
searching, no one. Could I have forgot
that he was dead? "Dad?" I cried out
again. For it was an impossible situation.
We were supposed to have gone fishing.
Get an early start. Be an early bird. He
was going to teach me how to dive in, swim.
I heard that thunder and the sound of rain,
so goodbye that plan. But there he was at
the breakfast table, looking white as a swan.
"Flakes?" he asked, and rose he and began
preparing my breakfast, my flakes in a bowl,
milk, toast and jam. As I ate I stared at
him, still naked in his shorts, why I could
almost see through him. "Dad, why are
you dead?" I asked him. But he made no
answer. "Dad?" I asked him again, anxious
to know why. "Dad?" Then there was only
his eyes, staring hard at me, wild. And then
there was no one, a clap of thunder, and he
was gone.

14 WAYS OF LOOKING AT
    MY FATHER

My father had a funny head, big and
hard and funny. I tried to hit him over
his big head once with a big rock once,
and the rock broke in half as my father
smiled and said, "Huh?" Ears too big
and independent, nose prominent and
flattened, I suppose, by many adolescent
skirmishes, and a jaw that supported the
rest. He's tall. Dark hair with olive skin.
An evil mustache, I think. Intense black
eyes you don't want to look into for too
long without going blind, yeah, I said it,
blind. I've seen compassion inside of
them, like when I've broken something
and stand waiting for a beating. I've seen
anger and despair. I've seen neediness.
"C'mere," he'll say, "and hold me hard."
I've seen an eight years old boy with a
bicycle riding away, far fast away, and
my father shouting, "Come back, you little
devil, come back here!" I've seen distance.
But there's nobody can really know what
I've seen. Nobody but me, and I'd mostly
rather forget it, if you know what I mean.
Tattoos, I almost forgot, from wrist to chest
to shoulders, snakes and dragons, with just
a couple of falling stars, look out! thrown in.

UNTITLED BLUE-EYED FRED

On one road there was Fred & Fred
Fred had blue eyes Fred had & Fred had
always thought of himself as a blue-eyed
& hugely handsome actually heavenly Fred

I can't stop thinking about him Fred
but I can I must & I can. For just to
stare into the blue eyes of blue-eyed Fred
Fred had blonde hair too. Fred's hair

but aren't you tired by now of him Fred
let's just climb a bit down here & around
there & my goodness there's Fred sitting on a
Fred of all things inhuman & there's Fred

tiny scar on his forehead & his wet lips wet
as if he was thinking of but what could a wet
Fred be thinking of his lips set jaw set I sometimes
do wish I could ask him Fred whatever are you

thinking of whatever are you thinking of oh Fred

THEM

So this is my family, yes, the dreaded Them.
This was taken years before I was even born.
I didn't have any real style then, so I wore
my cute white sailor zoot and red and blue bow-
tie. Was I truly the little monster I grew up
to be? We've all gathered because it's my birth-
day, it's my 79th, that was long ago and not so
far away. My mother is as pretty as a movie
star as I sneak into midnight beds beside her
who dies in my arms. My older sister the rose
in my arms. She's always laying on the couch
in her pink slip, reading, reading, as I play
with my guns. She's not pretty pretty like me,
but she's not ugly ugly either, but neither am I.
"Say, whatcha doing, Sis?" I ask her. "I'm just
reading," she says. "Whatcha reading, Sis?" I ask her.
"Words," she says, "pretty words." "I know them
words, Sis" I tell her. "You do? Then write me a
poem!" "What's a poem, Sis, huh?" I ask her. But
she never ever answers. But I vow that someday I
shall find the answer to what is a poem, oh yeah,
someday, Sis, someday. My brother, why he died
oh shoot in my arms, so goodbye Bro, I miss you so.
Mother, she tells me not to run around wild like I
do. "You wild Indian!" she tells me. But I don't
care. I like to run wild with the wind. I like to go
bang bang. No, I was never that old, was I? Impossible
life, my lives, loves, old dreams, my voices of
a dusty gravel, keep singing, he keeps, he keeps,
my dear father, he keeps staring at me, as if
he's always wondering who in the hell I am, and
where in the damn devil did I come from? "I come
from heaven, Papa" it's I do like to remind him, every
now and then, but he I wonder why but he never blinks.

THE GREAT PRETENDER

I like to pretend. Are you a pretender, too? Sometimes, I just like to
lie back and play with my thoughts, such as they are, but shadows
and dust. I like to let my fingers fly up into air, and there I am: 2
birds. One is a he bird and the other is a she bird, and they fly and
they fly all over the sky, to alight on a tree where they quick do the
nasty, tweet tweet, and then they fly away on the Starship Enterprise,
keep our country free. Me, I was born, eeks, on May 31st in 1931,
and on that night my mama she held me high up high in the air. "Hey,
you there, you gonna be trouble?" she asked me. And then I nodded
my little head (so she said) and I answered, "Shore am. Shore am." I
remember the Bronx. 835 East 152nd Street. Remember lots of people
who babysat me and let me run around crazy while my parents were
working, from the super in the basement, an old Polish man, where
I'd nap on his cot as he went muttering on about his work, or I'd run
around crazy and dream big dreams. I'd somehow be rich was one.
We had neighbors who were devout Catholics and when they went
to church, they'd take me, and I sure liked the idea of Jesus and God,
his Dad. Oh, I made my Bar Mitzvah when I was 13, but I sure did
like Jesus, Lord help me. PS 25, where I studied George Washington,
how he could not tell a lie, cherry pie. And Abe, Abraham Lincoln,
Honest Abe. Lincoln Hospital, where I had my tonsils taken out, my
poor sore throat, and all the ice cream I was allowed, at last! to have. I
remember her voice, my English teacher, as she read to us Walt Whit
man, "When lilacs last bloomed." Hunts Point Avenue. Southern
Boulevard. Fox Street, where I, maybe 14, 15, sat on the ledge of our
window, 6th floor, thinking for sure that I was a fag and bad and this
is the Bronx and we don't like bad fags. So-o did I jump? You tell me.
Pelham Bay Park, where on summer weekends my parents met with
our other relatives, all immigrants, and there under the wavy trees,
they'd eat and weep and sing songs about their dear old lost Mother
Russia. And I, could I ever go back, back to my way lost Bronx again?

12 or 13, I had scarlet fever, left me weak and weaker. My mother, when I had nearly recovered, would take off from work and she'd take me to the pier near the East River to breathe in the salt air. There, we'd just sit, she and I, and we'd talk or just not talk, and we'd listen to the lapping of the waters and we'd smell that river smell, how I really love that smell. And I felt how she really loved me deeply and was worried about me, my little life, my future. "Don't you worry, Ma," I'd say. "Cause I'll be a poet," I'd say. "A famous poet, Ma. Like that guy Walt Whitman. And I'll be so rich, yeah, you'll see, Ma, some sweet sweet day."

GRANDMA

Yeah, I like to dance. Hey, look Ma, I'm
dancing! My grandma was a good little
dancer, eh? I told my grandma she was
my dancing princess, & my grandma she
just shrugged & said oh you shove it. Snow
fell like fairy sparkles over our burning house,
& my dear little grandma she just laughed &
she laughed & danced us kids over the coals,
& she spit & she spit all over our burnt parts,
putting me out, oh she the fairy queen of my
burning heart. Pa said to keep away from that
old woman, she's crazy, & maybe she was &
just maybe I am, too, yes I am crazy, crazy, eh?
But Pa he was just afraid of her, all her burning
candles & her bed forever unslept in. One night,
Grandma, she kept sprouting branches & pretty
leaves of all kinds & colors, & so I'd climb &
I'd climb them & all her many breasts of such
pretty flowers, & I'd touch all these things oh
I'd never touched in those far forests before, &
so then we danced, my little grandma & little me,
around & around & around, we danced & danced.

Of course it was love. Eleanor (on
the bottom right) loved to go on picnics.
Below: Assistant Secretary of the Navy
Mr. Roosevelt reviewing the Victory Fleet
on its return from Europe, December, 1918.
Eleanor is second from the left. Theodore
Roosevelt considered Bob Ferguson one
of the bravest men he had ever known,
and some of Eleanor's friends suspected
that she once had had a romantic interest
in him. Below: The notification ceremony
at Hyde Park, August 9, 1920, after FDR
had been nominated for vice president. Be-
low, 1907: Anna, now a one-year old, with
her two delighted parents. The dog's name
was Duffy.

HOME MOVIES

Let me sing. Yes I have done wrong but dang it.
It's how to teach light & turning moving on. I
mean I almost think that these tiny city gardens
and there you are, and your face above me, burning
burning. I mean if you want to live in the jungle why
why even then. Hello dawn and longing, longing.
And is it noon now, and am I in love, you terrible
thing? Myself, I am the bad one, I am, I am that
promiscuous every five minutes for that I live
on a farm on Mars. Our hearts our hunger our very
red children our human pain. It's really a lovely
feeling really lovely. The huskiness of a dusk
that we know them we who other flowers have
crushed by paws of hungry lovers treading oh tygers tygers
yearning oh so lightly home. Your bodies consisting of
I lick me a little warm milk and I say my nightly prayers
    oh star of stars
    oh promises to come
    oh now will you love
Our hearts our precious water our very children our queer
when the so-called normal world beckons, yes I hear
and I shall come. Oh when we ourselves were all of a
jungle I sing I sink of our pretty hearts boxes, what now
shall hold our pale Dinah flowers, our whispering pines?
Yes, I do have to stop writing these so sad things for these
    so real sweethearts to read. Yes and
yes, I do and am one lone starling sings of the reddest sunsets
delicious you delicious of beings. Eve as she awakens and
sees in her palm the pale green frog of a sleeping young prince,
turns, purses her lips, and bends for a kiss, just once more, one more kiss.

ELEVEN

"I'm eleven today!" I sang, and so I ran out
into the sunshine. Then, a big brown horsie
came riding, with a big man upon it, who smiled
and stared down upon me. "Whoa, boy," he said,
"and where are you off running?" "I'm eleven
today, sir, and I'm eleven!" "Well, good for you,
boy!" he said. "And for my birthday gift to you,
I'll let you pet my horse!" And so I did, and the
horsie neighed and nuzzled me a little as I pet it.
"Well, we're off now, Mister Eleven, to defend the
world, but you have a nice safe day!" And the nice
horsie galloped away. In the park, why there's a
lady in a grass skirt dancing, of all things, dancing,
what a wonderful day! "Hello, lady," I say, but she
keeps on dancing and dancing, away, away. There's
a dog comes up to me, so thin, looks hungry. "Hello,
doggie, doggie," I say. "You hungry, huh? You
lost? You hungry?" But the doggie just gives out
one whimper, and scurries away. "Come back!" I
say, and "Come back!" But the doggie's away, far
gone away. There's a bird flies onto a tree, and so
I say, "Hello, little birdie, and I'm eleven, and hello
there, tree!" But the birdie just cocks its head at me
for a minute, and then flies away without even one
sweet tweet. "Goodbye, little bluebird!" I hear my-
self saying, and I think I'm crying. Yes, I am crying.
I'm eleven and I am crying. "But why are you
crying?" I hear a voice asking. Is it the tree? Can a
tree really be talking just to me? Then I see it's my
mother. "Why on earth are you crying?" It's an-
other voice asking? Is it the horsie or the little lost
doggie? Or is it the tree? No, it's my father. "You

are eleven now, my sonnie," he says. "And a boy of eleven shouldn't cry," he says, staring down at me. "No, I won't cry, Papa," I say, drying my eyes. "I won't ever cry," I say, "not ever. Because I'm eleven. And I won't ever cry again!" "Then let's all go home," mother says. And, taking my hand, we all walk away back, back home.

THE PARK NEAR CLOSING

One used condom. No. Two. What
a place. This boy looks at me as if to
say, "Who the hell are you?" I wish I
could tell you, kid, if I only knew. One
crushed can of Mountain Dew, rather
pretty. Oh no, two. Do they talk to
one another as they lie there? Once, I
was young and full of juice, now I'm
just like ugh you. A pretty girl with a
camera, she looks at me, yes, take my
picture, I can smile, see, see how I smile?
but she quick looks away, away. From
nowhere, somewhere, there drifts a song,
a rather sad song, and the singer: "You'd
better go now…" and I should, but I don't.
There's an old bench stained with yes-
terday's teardrops and, a little weary, I just
must sit down.

MOON

I do like the word. Moon. "Moon," I say,
and as I say it I see it, oh my beauty, just as day
light fades into moon, a tilted moon, I see you,
oh moon, see me. I'm not myself tonight, but
soon oh moon do see me as I walk alone along
your very cusp in this evening's hush, and was I
dreaming? am I so lost again somewhere in a
dream? and am I always babe naked? and babbling
crazily to no one, a curious loon. There's always
a crazy guy like me walking slowly along the
ever darkening street, just an ordinary guy like,
say, me, and trying to hide his fear by whistling.
But who am I frightened of? no, not you, moon.
But yes, for I thought I saw a shadow on the moon,
was just the shadow of a man, that's who, and that's
all it was, he was just walking along, whistling in
the dark, the dark of the moon, just walking along.

TONGUES

Stevens forces the stable hand's
head down with his black gloved hands
and roughly stuffs it into Hunt's mouth
fun, no? Those big muscular horses
britches and boots sleep in, too. Golden
earth-evening light bathes the humble
cell of my room, and then sidles up and
alongside each of his muscular flanks.
Oopsie! They've woken up the stable
master who, like some cruel, tattooed
piece of machinery that pounds and pounds
until you just become lust delirious and
continues on until there you are and you
you are babbling away and away in tongues

THIS IS NOT MY HOUSE

yet I keep walking past it
and past it. Once I saw what
I thought was a face in a window
but when I looked again
and again, I looked and I looked
but there was no one. "What's
happened to you?" I called out
but the house simply seemed to sigh
and that was that. No one. Nothing.
"Are you more
than bricks and mortar?" I asked it
one midnight, standing before it
I don't know why. Of course, there
was no answer. It's not my house
and never was. Wonder whose house
it was.

SENSE AND SENSIBILITY

I live with memories
of this guy. This guy,
he was always reading.
I guess he really lived
between the covers of
the many books he loved.
Those books were his real
lovers. Oh, he and I, we
once one night we made
love, but he kept on reading
even as we did. And, when
I looked up, I saw it was Sense
and Sensibility he was reading.
Written by Miss Jane Austen.
I didn't mind. I just wanted
him so much. But his eyes
always so sad, and I had to
wonder why and whatever for?
He lived once on my floor, just
right across the hall, but now he
doesn't live there, not anymore.

THIS DAY

What a day. I awake. I awoke. And then, you
might ask, what happened? Lord knows. One
sigh, they tell me, is all we're allowed, and
then the hour: noon, afternoon, evening, when
one just murmurs, "Be kind." Now light fades
into moon, a tilted moon, I see you, oh moon,
see me. I seem to be naked as a loon at this very
moment, and talking crazy, but to who, excuse
me, I meant to whom? Well, there was a gentle-
man, but he's dressed and gone, my heart, he's
gone. And I believe he was writing a book, but
who in this forsaken city isn't? I mean, come on.
And we spoke, when we spoke, of time, time
endlessly passing, not a pleasant conversation,
but that is my past, and the gentleman's gone.
And now, I suppose I should sleep, moon, and
what do you think? but soon sleep leads to dream,
and dream tends to shoot me bolt awake with a
bit of a scream, and there I am, naked and wet
and glistening as the day was born. Was I falling
again, falling into you, moon? No, no answer,
but yes I shall dress and go out to greet you, hello
again, moon.

PROMISE

I vowed to you I would.
Did you send me this poem, Mom?
Did you wake to find yourself a son
who was almost, but not quite, a man?
He listens to her listening her way of
ever so slowly breathing sinking in breathing.
We put you in a place, but we have always
put you in a place. "It's hard to read here,"
once you quietly complained. "I think
here they steal things. My golden slippers.
My dancing shoes." I see you dance.
Is that you dancing? What movie
was that from, as the pretty music began
and up we sprang? And so we danced our
selves round and around, and I in my so tiny
blue boy pajamas, and you in your night of
white gown. No, I only remember that moon.
"Yes, Mom," I said, "I'll be your good boy,
from now on."

IN THE ROOM

There was nothing in the room except the tree.
Then I came. So the room held the tree and me.
Well, I needed a lamp to read by, didn't I? So
the room held me and the lamp and the tree.
"My, my," I thought, "but it's beginning to get
a bit crowded in here. It's beginning to be a city."
And soon a duck came waddling in and sat down,
exhausted, right on me. "If I could please see the
sky?" I told it. So I got up and "Excuse me," I
said to the duck, and I went to the door and I
opened it ever so slightly for just a tiny peek.
Goodness, the sky was so beautiful I almost tipped
over. Full of drifting pink clouds and the bluest of
birds, as blue as the sea. Was that an angel winging
right toward me? So, I closed the door quickly and
went back into it, in the room, but by then, besides
the lamp and the tree, there was a bed and a stove
and, on it, something was cooking, but what? And
then came a woman, very angry yet very beautiful,
goodness me. "Where on earth have you been, my
sweet handsome husband and my one true love?
For I've been looking all over the room for you!
Dinner, my darling, is ready. It's a delicious duck
soup, feathers and all, and I've been cooking it for
forever and ever, love, so let's do sit down and eat."
Well, of course I did, we did, we sat and we ate
and we ate and we ate. And it was so delicious, her
delicious duck soup, that we ate the forks and the
knives and we ate the spoons, and then, of course,
we ate the delicious plates. And then, of course,
we ate each other, even if it took all night and far
far into the sweet bright day.

White gardenias, worn in her hair, became Billie Holiday's trademark.
I like to read the great poet Frank O'Hara's great poem, "The Day
Lady Died," as often as I can. In 1937, Billie received her nickname
"Lady Day" from sax player Lester Young. I saved, and in 1948 I got
a ticket to see Lady Day live at Carnegie Hall, and I fell in love, deep-
est love. It was like, song after song, she was singing secrets, such
beautiful, terrible secrets. How did she do that? Could I ever ever do
that? "Don't threaten me with love, baby. Let's just go walking in the
rain." In 1959, Billie Holiday died at the age of 44. On a rainy night
in 1951, I went to the Palace Theater to see Judy. Judy who? Miss
Judy Garland a/k/a little Dorothy from Kansas and Oz. And it was my
tragic love again. For her closing number, Judy sat in her clown outfit,
feet dangling over the edge of the stage, and sang "Over The Rainbow."
"If happy little bluebirds fly/beyond the rainbow/why oh why…???" I
cried. On June 22, 1969, Judy Garland died in London, England. Did
the shocking news of her death touch off the Stonewall Riots? She
males & tee hee males running wild in the streets, and free? Why
oh why? Bunny Berrigan died. Freddie Martin died. Gene Krupa's
mother tried to persuade him to become a priest instead of pursuing
a career in music. A German woman named Holloway taught Count
Basie piano for 25 cents a lesson. The Freddie Martin Orchestra began
touring regularly in 1931, the year I was born. In 1941, and at the age
of 10, I was just beginning to feel sort of quote "different" unquote.
Would I grow up to be, horrors, a pervert? Or, extra horrors of hor-
rors, a poet? In 1936, Duke Ellington received the keys to the city of
Los Angeles. Sidney Bechet played clarinet and soprano sax. Sidney
Bechet died May 14, 1959, in Paris, France. A lot of black musicians
drifted over to Paris, France. It was just easier, I guess, America. But
before they were lost and gone forever, I saw me the big bands, I did,
yes me, crazy gay kid. I'd bring me a sandwich or two and I'd sit all
day at the Strand Theater, The Capitol Theatre or The Paramount The-
atre, NYC, and I saw The Stan Kenton Band rise out of the pit, I saw

the Dorsey Brothers, Jimmy and Tommy, I saw Benny Goodman with Gene Krupa on drums, playing "Sing Sing Sing." I saw Red Norvo and Mildred Bailey, and her theme song was "Ole Rockin' Chair." All those theme songs, all those theme songs. Saw Woody, Woody Herman and His Herd, saw Mr. Les Brown and His Band of Renown with Doris Day. I waited and I got Louis Prima's autograph. Louis Prima, he signed my autograph book: "Be Happy." He looked at me, trembling up at him, smiled and signed my book: "Be Happy." And he signed it: Louis Prima. Glen Miller, lost, lost in the war! And just like that, the Big Band era was over, and so was my wild wild dissolute youth. Lady Day, Billie Holiday died. Judy, Miss Garland, goodbye. Chick Webb's last words were, "I'm sorry, I gotta go now." But I still hear you, Billie: "You'd better go now, because I love you much too much, you have a way with you…" And oh, Billie, I still do. I still love you. I love you. Love you.

SLEEP

For a long time I used to go to bed early.
For one thing, comes a time at night when
I can't look anymore at my room. My room
full of dust and vapors, my paper room, for I
am made of pen and ink and it's hard to remember
when it all began and was all over in but a blink.
For a long time I wondered if I was going
to be able to keep it and then it was gone, so I
went to bed early to sleep. When your room
falls apart, you're either out on the street or
fast asleep. For a long time I would meet
men and go to their apartments just to see their
rooms and a few of their rooms they were pretty
nice places where a guy could sit naked and
stare out at trees and where soft other voices would
filter in with words like "bread" and "cheese" till
I got so sleepy I would have to say "excuse me"
and go home, no matter how early, and just to sleep,
just to throw myself into my bed and just go peep,
right off into sleep, a deep deep sleep, blessed sleep.

BING

No I never got it. No, once you missed it, it's
gone. So he wound up driving us around and
stuff, getting drunk. Not sure I'm not sure I
should be telling you this, but somewhere he
stops the car and we sit there and suddenly he
says Georgie. I don't say nothing. He says
Georgie again. Then he says Georgie Porgie.
Then he says How old are you now? I says 13
next month. He says next month next month.
He says 13 and then he says it again, 13. Says
That's a good age an okay age 13. What chew
gonna be huh? The fucking excuse my English
President huh? The king of the fucking excuse
my English empire? Georgie Porgie Pudding
and Pie huh? You gonna grow off to college
huh Mister Pie? I says I don't think so I suck
excuse my English at math for one fuck thing,
Uncle Bing. He says Math? He says fuck it
fuck Math huh Georgie fuck Math! I says
Yeah yeah fuck math! He says Ya just gotta
sit your ass down and study Buddy study.
Me I never studied hard enough worth a shit
so that's how come I wind up a butt nothing
nobody who is thinking of shoving a gun up
my stupid butt and pulling the trigger goodbye
now huh bye bye. So I think for a while while
we sit there quiet cars whizzing by god fuck.
Then I says Don't go do that Uncle Bing. He
says No? I says No. He says Why not? I says
You'll upset the whole apple cart. He says The
apple cart? And he laughs and says The apple
cart one more time laughs and guns the motor

and then off we go to home. We can go fishing
maybe tomorrow Georgie Porgie. We can wake
up earlier so we catch the boat. Why you fucking
miss the boat why that's it it's gone. So let's
get you home little birthday next month boy and
we'll try it again huh? We'll try it again. And
so, just like that, we went gone. We went gone.

HOW TO END THE WAR you start by

folding sweet poetry to fold into envelopes
to mail to a street in Iraq or a star in your ear
alright everybody say the war is over ok?
but no the war is not over so now don't say
alright you alone Kid you can say the wawa
it but yet I was never quite sure what to sink
do or what to say He would say that perhaps
He never walked the earth it was a darling
little box it was like a truly felt hat it was all
most like a feeling that it was that darlink
felt & funny how the 2 men agreed one was
Hi call me Absence & one was just call me
Fonder. What's my job? I am poet/pervert I
work with a pen & a penis it is my penis writing
all this shit but then he decided he was really
pissed off at the National Fucking Endowment
For The Academical Farts it was a gay bar up
uptown of all these silently Asian men & I
I could never really figure out what on earth
was I doing there but still there I was & yet
tell me I mean what was I doing there was I gay?
was I Asian? so what am I doing in this here war?
& then the year of it went by & somehow it was
time to move on eat something like resembling
food that really all happened & then we I really
mean he & I met it was somewhere on Prince
Street & I thought he was gorgeous & he sorta
turned & he sorta saw me was I looking perhaps in
a sorta window? for indeed they have interesting
windows there on Prince Street if you ask me.

"If ever you need a friend," he wrote in
my yearbook, "you can depend on me."
He was the school jock, he was. I never
could figure out exactly why we were
friends, except he had to see how much I
liked him. He was wearing cut-off blue
jeans, a white tank top, white knee socks
and white sneakers, and for the life of me
I couldn't breathe. I was both afraid of
him and vaguely thrilled by him, as we
stood on his roof in the sunshine, looking
down over the city. "Making you dizzy?
It's hard to look at it, ain't it?" he asked.
"Huh?" I asked, and repeated again, "huh?"
"It's this city," he went on, "this damn scary
city." Then he quick took off his tank top and
he just stood half-naked before me. And I just
wanted to jump. Off of the rooftop, just jump
it. Maybe I'd fly or maybe not, and you tell
me so what? He just made my eyes hurt bad.
"Look at me," he said, his face very serious.
"What do you think?" he asked, standing
right before me. "Tell me," he said, leaning
in to me. "And be honest. Even if it hurts.
Just tell me. Tell me what in hell you think."

MY LOVE LIFE

I am intent on improving my love life
& to squeeze the receptacle end to release any
of the penis, as the sperm can be released
against the penis at the ring area of the testy
penis. Store penis at room temperature, please
& do not expose penis to the light for when light
hits the penis the penis may my goodness break dance for joy
which joy can increase the potential for breakage. Breakage
bad. Baaad. & then, pretty soon, Bub, comes the Spring
& with Spring comes, you know what I'm saying? Spring,
Spring! when a young man's heart & hand beats faster & ever ever
faster! Say, is this the Empire State Building I have my hairy hand
wrapped around, & are you King Kong? Well, well, hello there, Mister Kong.

I'LL BE SEEING YOU

I remember when
I'll Be Seeing You
Poems 1962-1976
by Larry Fagin &
published by
Full Court Press
cost me $3.50 when I
bought it & read it
& liked it really liked it
back in 1976
when I had a lot of sex
I don't know why ex
cept it was 1976 & I
just stood in the window
just sort of naked
& I had a lot of sex
but that was 1976 & then
came 1980 & then
came 1990 & then
came 2000 & now it's
2010 & early August it's
August 6, 2010 & here
I sit reading
I'll Be Seeing You
by Larry Fagin
again
& I still like it
so-o well
whadya know & son
of a gun

MASON

Mason, of course, drops to his knees, while
Kurt, of course, mutters something about never
all while standing on one leg like a pink flamingo
looking for love online. Does he have a huge thingo
for Mr. Postman, or is it hey hey just us? Looking
like the cat that just swallowed the canary, Kevin,
you know him, comes in and comes in and comes in.
Mormon missionary? Census taker? The Second
Coming? We'll sigh never know. Dreamboat Maxx
up in the window does his special tongue flute dance.
So which one is the straight guy, you ask? Beats us.
And who cares because delicious and vulpine, duh,
Rocky is in need of a shower. The water fetchingly
pounds on his Call Me Jim and drips down his manly
sins to be lost forever in that crazee gushing LaLa-land
river of no return. Ah, innocence! goodbye forever
and so so looooong!

SKULLS & STUFF

Hello this is me & my skull,
& so hello. Words Words Words
Words. So I guess this is my
poem about my skull. I was a
beautiful girl once, happy as a
princess in a castle. You ask me
what my name was, but I don't
remember, for that was so long ago
before Time began, & now I am no
one, oh just another skull. Perhaps
we can chat a bit more, perhaps way
later on, about Time & longing,
but that's another song. We lived
by a flowing stream & my father
was King & my mother The Queen.
More Words, says my sweet pet,
Pugnose the parrot, who they buried
beside me, my Puggy, while outside
the wars did rain. "Let's you & me
do it," said the Indian Chief, as he
fondled my beautiful breasts with
his huge wondrous hard-on. "Would
you like to do it?" he asked me, as
it began to rain, and so yes we did,
yes, the rain makes a girl so want to.
"Let love rain!" my Chief began to chant
above me, while kissing me most fiercely.
Oh words the heat from his hot fucking
body, why it almost burned me! for I
was then but a delicate flower to be sure.
I said, "I think, my Chief, I'm a coming,
oh you terrible savage!" as I came &

I came. Words Words Words Words.
& now I am just but a skull, but I have
my memories, oh my night of nights.
So folks please remember to smile, even
though it hurts, & especially when it
rains, oh remember me then, if only in
passing, how a shy nameless girl loved the
falling of the rain. So I guess, hello &
goodbye, that this is farewell & The End.

APRIL

As gently as she could, she slowly lifted the
sheet and slid into the bed next to her friend,
April. They both lay on their backs, their
bare bodies almost touching, not really, but
almost. She thought how almost perfect it
was, this exquisite torture of so close, yet so
far. How April's cruelly perfect nude body
twisted, hands above her head, as if in the
very throes of sex. Yes, she sniffed, yes it was
there, the heady smell of sex between them,
hanging thick in the air. In a few minutes, she
knew she would have to leave this precious bed
with its precious cargo, her cruel April, and return
to her own bed, where she knew she wouldn't
sleep, alone with her visions, alone with her need.

CHARLIE

After speaking with his mother, Charlie
slowly hung up the phone, and began to
cry. He didn't know what else to do with
his feelings. Then, after a while, he began
to wonder, and he dialed. "Hi, Mom," he
said, "it's me again. I was just wondering.
Are you crying, too?" There was a slight pause,
and then her voice, soft and breathy, "Yes,
Charlie. I am crying, dear. How did you
know?" "Because I could hear you," he
answered, and she laughed. "Oh, my funny
boy," she said. "Wait! Wait!" she quickly
added, and walked into the kitchen, turning on
the water. "I'm cooking," she said. "What are
you cooking, Mom?" he asked. "Spaghetti,
Charlie. Spaghetti and meatballs. Your favorite."
"Sounds good," he said. "Can I come over?"
"From all the way over where you are?" she asked.
"All the way from over there?" "I'd swim all the
way, Mom, for your spaghetti and meatballs."
"My funny boy," she said again, and then, after a
slight pause, "Well, then, I'll set a place for you,
and I'll wait. I'll be waiting, Charlie, you hear me?"
"Yeah, Mom. I hear you." he said, and almost
whispered. And she quickly hung up. "See you,"
Charlie said, and then he just began crying again.

HUMMER

"I'll tell you nothing," he said, as we drove along.
I could almost count the poles as we sped along.
And my father hummed. He was a hummer. I
looked up and saw the clouds holding up the sky.
"You're not gonna see me," my father said, "once
we get there." And then he sort of chuckled, a
funny sound. "I mean," he went on, "that I am
just gonna disappear." Ahead, I saw a kid on the
side of the highway, holding out his thumb. The
kid looked hot. The sun was out and it was hot.
I could see he was almost soaking wet in sweat.
My father just drove by. "You could've stopped
for him, Dad," I said. "It would've been like a nice
thing to do." Immediately, my Dad stopped the
car, and we both lurched forward, then back. "You
wanna get out and walk it?" he queried. I thought
about it and swallowed. "No, sir, I don't." "Don't
what?" "Don't wanna walk it, sir." He stared hard
at me for one long minute. I could see the cactus,
sky and the mountains in the far far distance, as he
kept on staring. I could see the kid sort of running
in a funny hop towards us, my father's car. "So
do we understand each other from now on?" my
father asked me. "Do we understand each other at
last?" Thick silence, and I had to answer. "Yes, sir,
Dad." "Yes, sir, what, boy? I said yes, sir, what?"
"Sir, we understand each other at last." My father's
arms shot up as if in a weird kind of victory. "At
last!" he said, almost breathless. "At last!" By now,
the kid had almost reached the car, and he had one
arm out as if to quick grab at the handle of it, my

father's sky blue car. And I could see the kid's eyes,
kind of crazy scared eyes. "Good," my father said,
as he gunned the motor, and away we drove real fast.

MY DAD

My Dad comes from a long line of farmers.
All the vegetables he's raised they're good
for you, healthy and nutritious and delicious.
Being a farmer is hard work and think of that.
My Dad had rough hands, the hands of a
rough man. Broad shoulders my Dad would
hike me up upon and we'd go riding. I'd go
Hup Hup and my Dad would neigh like a
wild wild horse would neigh, and off we'd go
riding, wild and away. Or I'd stand and I'd
watch him as he walked on his hands, around
and around and around, there he goes, my Dad,
he's my father the farmer, walking like a king
on his hands. Some nights, we'd look in his
book of pictures of mountains, Mount This,
Mount That, Mount Everest, and my Dad he'd
go, "Now wouldn't you like to climb it?" and
then he'd point to the very top of that mountain.
And he'd say, "Son, I can see you up there,
right there at the very top, and waving away.
Waving to me, your very proud Dad!" I'd say,
"Dad but Dad, it looks up so high. I'd get all
dizzy And it looks so cold and icy, why I'd
slip and slide my sorry ass off all the way down,
ouch ouch, way way down!" And my Dad he
would always laugh and grab me and hold me
with his big rough hands to his great broad
chest, "Oh yes, that's you on the very top of it,
waving away, waving at me, your own Dad,
way down below. Yes, you, son. Waving at
me."

BACK DOOR MAN

Me, I'm a back door man. Are you?
I carry the last cardboard suitcase face
of earth. He left her and her cat purring
goodnight, sleep tight, goodnight. The wind
wrapped itself around him like the saddest
thought, and he began to cry. "Oh moon!"
he cried. He remembered his dead father
standing over him in his white white boxers
dead of night. "Why oh why are you
crying tonight?" his father, staring hard
down at him and asking why. "Because
nobody loves me!" he cries to his angry
father. "Because you don't love me!" he
cries to his father. "You!" He could barely
peek through the gap in his father's boxers
at his father's penis, and it looked so dark,
deep and forbidden that the very thought
of it only made him cry the harder. "Of
course nobody loves you," his father told
him, bending close to his ear. "Nobody
loves a little sissy boy crying for nothing.
For nothing!" His angry father getting into
bed beside him. His father taking him into
his arms. The very smell of him, his father,
so deep in his arms. And he could see the
moon in the bureau mirror, round and full.

BALLOON

Hello. I'm a sword-swallower. Are you
a sword-swallower, too? They'd laugh
at us, you know. Once, at the fair, on a
windy Sunday, I saw a child, a funny little
boy, lose hold of a balloon, a red balloon,
and so off it went into the dark blue, long
string and all, and I had to turn my eyes
away, as the little boy began to cry for his
lost balloon, oh no, oh no. "I'll get you
another," said his impatient father, but the
little boy kept on pointing to the sky and
he kept on crying for his lost red balloon.

Even today, I sometimes wonder where's
that little boy now, for that was years and
years ago, and by now the little boy must be
all grown. Does he ever think of his lost
balloon, and does the thought make him cry
again? And where has the juggler who was
once my lover gone, his thick cardboard
suitcase, plates in air, and his swift hands?
I would sometimes double as a clown, my
garish whiteface, rubber nose, blood red lips
painted on, all to make you children laugh
and scream before the sun was gone, and
then the hungry lions, have I told you of the
lions, the hungry lions, who come roaring on?

THE LITTLE DEER

The witch said, "The deer! The little deer! Run
after the deer and capture him, my little darling,
and you shall be king!" So I did what the witch
told me. I ran and I ran, but that little deer was a
fast one, and always leaped ahead, just out of reach.
Suddenly, there I was, in the heart of the forbidden
forest, and I was alone, for the little deer was gone.
"Who is that under me?" asked the talking tree.
"It's me," I answered, "your little king." "You're not
my little king!" replied the tree. "You're just a lost
and frightened little boy, aren't you? Afraid that
someone will eat you? Afraid you'll never find your
way back home?" "Yes, tree," I said, for it was true.
"Climb a bit up me, little boy, and I'll try to protect
you. I'll try to find someone to guide you out of this
forest you are lost within." Just then, a riderless
white horse came along. "Oh dear me, oh dear me,"
said the sad horse. "For the Prince of this strange
kingdom and I went out riding, but the Prince he
strangely fell off me, he fell to the ground where he
is now unconscious, and I can't wake him for the
life of me, oh dear!" "Then let this little boy ride on
you, and take him where the strange Prince lies. I do
believe the boy has the magic to wake the Prince up!"
So there I was, riding on the white horse. "Hold me
tight, boy!" the horse commanded, and soon there we
were before the sleeping Prince. "Do your magic,
boy!" the horse whispered. So I bent over the Prince
who was so handsome why I kissed him on his lips, and
that kiss seemed to do it. The Prince awoke and lifted
his head toward me. "Is it you, boy?" he asked. "Yes,"

I said, "oh yes!" "You've saved me, boy! Why I was
lost in a dream of wolves and dragons!" "It was my duty
and my honor, sir!" "Then come and we shall ride back
to my kingdom, boy, and you shall stay at my side forever,
for who knows when I shall need that magic kiss again!"
And so it came true, for I find there is no denying the
command of a handsome Prince. Could I? Could you?

CHIWAWAS

Did you know chiwawas are descended
from wolves? Do not get a chiwawa mad at
you or he'll bite your head off and eat it for
lunch. I saw a chiwawa eat a sheep once,
and then knit himself a sweater with the
leftover wool. He says you got a secret.
A chiwawa can tell if you got a secret. A
chiwawa can smell your secret in you, and
spell it out. "I'm gonna tell on you, sucka,"
my chiwawa whispers when we go for a walk.
Sometimes I just wanna kill my naughty chiwawa,
but I love my little Chi Chi too much. At night, as
we sleep together, and he howls at the moon in
my ear, I just wanna kiss him all over, my sweet
little sweetheart Chi Chi, my very darling dear.

LILI MARLENE

These streets, these rooms, these soldiers.
One guy plays from a dusty accordion, what
a gloomy old place. No one dances. I sit
on a bench. In a moment, I will ask him,
Gunther, to dance with me. There are no
women left for us, so why not dance, he and
I together, to Lili Marlene? A bottle of wine
and a rather sad little song, shuffling round
and around? Later, outside, after we kiss and
he grins and spits, "Let's go for some Chinese,
baby!" and suddenly his arm around me, as if
we were buddies, old pals. We pass a comrade
lying dead on the sidewalk, face down in the
red red snow, his helmet askance. "It's Josef,"
I whisper. "Yeah, yeah Josef," he says, letting
out great breaths, "let's go." "We'll come back,
won't we?" I ask. "Maybe," he answers, spits,
and laughs. "And maybe not," he adds. "It's
war, baby. And who the fuck knows, huh? Does
anyone know?" As if in silent answer, snow, the
snow starts to fall again on us, the dead and the
damned. "Fuck," he says, "why even fight and die
for a country with such bad fucking weather, huh?"
Laughs. My soldier laughs. "You'll be my Lili,"
he mutters. "Tonight. All night. My Lili Marlene."

A HOUSE

He built a house he didn't understand,
nor did it him. How many rooms, dear
Sir, it wondered, will it take you? How
many windows must you see through
before you see you? How many doors
will you lock tight against the moony
wolves? I see how you toss as you sleep,
how afraid to dream, yet how you seem
quite normal, where's the truth you bring?
Did you leave it weeping on the empty train,
lost and alone to the very end of the line?
Did you stare at the conductor, hoping for
some answer from him when there was none?
Why's that rock in your hand, and where
will you throw it so it makes not a sound?
Why do you stand naked on your lawn at
midnight, staring up at your house of shadows,
as it stares back utterly aghast at you? Shall
I tell you the truth? the sad house wonders, shall
I even begin to dare to tell you the awful truth?

DANCE

Let me dance. I put my left foot up
and I leave it to chance. If it ever comes
down, then down it comes, and my dance
is over, yet there's always the chance.
There's something so weird about 2 men
dancing together, isn't there? And my arms
around you, and your arms round me.
When will you let go, always I wonder, as
you hum in my ear, no, you mumble, rather,
something sad and distant I can hardly
hear, as I listen to you breathe. Later, as I
watch you dance away, still mumbling God
knows what, I really want to call out, "Hey,
come back!" but I don't, for some reason,
I don't. The truth is, you wouldn't come
back anyway and, let's face it, I can hardly
blame you. I'm not that much of a dancer,
I have to admit. I'm not that good at it.
I get winded sort of whirling around. And
I don't like my feet off the ground. Don't
enjoy the feeling of the earth as it spins
away, and now you turn the corner, and now
you are gone, well bless me, all gone. I'm
really not a dancer, not at all. It's just that
when the music began, well, and there you
were, and the music began, it began.

He stood by himself, staring at the dawn
in a field of thorns. A happy bluebird flew
near him, and said, "Why, hi there, hand-
some, how you doing?" The startled cowboy
was so startled why he almost fainted, but
instead he told his horse, "Giddy yap!" and so
off they rode. "Someday," he said to the sun,
"why this land will be your land, and mined."
Twanging his guitar as he passed cactus, sage
and cactus, cactus and sage. He passed 2 buf-
falo making buffalo love, and tried not to look.
He passed 2 cowboys making cowboy love, and
tried not to look, yet did, he looked and looked.
He passed a man carving something out of the
stone, and asked him, "Whatcher making there,
partner?" and the man said, "Dead presidents,
sonny, dead presidents." He passed ghost town
after ghost town and had to shiver, scared. He
twanged his trusty guitar and he sang of Love,
of love lost and love found, and of all the many
many mysteries of Life. He rode Old Paint for
miles and miles and miles, and high into the sky.

I CONFESS

I confess I don't have an alibi. Yeah, I'm
a bum. My big toe bores holes in my socks
and soul. Sorry I am all the times I could not
be there, or be square. I had a job but went
out to lunch and so kept on walking. Then I
got myself drunk and wound up in a strange
bed, legs up, a mess. And then this sadness I
hid under the table and I wouldn't come out.
First my father died and I could have cried
but I was there for him that dark dark night.
Then my mother died and I could have cried
and I cried, oh yes, I cried. Then looked out the
window at you shoveling snow and I thought
how beautiful now. Sometimes the world
feels made of parchment, so just break off a
piece of it and sometimes a poem, hey look God
a poem. Then I just burn it and warm the room.
An holey old sweater, old friend, hello. Fell
in love, got married, got a job, changed jobs,
stared up at skies. Got stoned under a willow,
oh dear me, got divorced, got sober, made old
friends, read books, good books. A good book
is like a good friend you can curl up with on a
dark night, to have and to hold in your arms for
ever and forever, sleep tight.

WAR

Past sullen ghosts angry pumpkins
and there you are: waiting. You take my hand
we enter these ruins faint cries of fallen angels
only a peep of sky here, one lost frantic bird
screeching over quicksand, we lick at love
I keep closing my eyes, you are so frightening
and now it's time. A church bell tolls at dawn
3 camouflaged soldiers, guns cocked, staring
"Is the war over yet? Ain't the war over yet, man?"
and gone, they're gone. It's my lover's inevitable yawn
or just an impatient Venus. Is she bored with us?
and when I turn again there's another face in your hand
and another you mumbling some golden butterfly's song
and I should, I think, be home. Fly home, little songbird, home.

LAST NIGHT

Last night, I saw the thousands
making love, the thousands crying
for love, and I, too, wanted to
weep, for my bed was awake, and I
could not sleep. I dressed and
went out into the streets, dark and
empty, and I walked and I walked,
miles of pain and waste, "please
release this devil who has taken me
over, body and soul, so I can go home
and find some peace!" It began to rain,
and I cupped my hand out and swallowed the
rain down thirstily, when I saw of a sudden
all the other hands moving around me,
men, women, even the children, reaching
into the dark of this dank wet city, all, all
grabbing for the rain, all for just one
swallow of the precious liquid, and thus
my loneliness was lifted in a moment and
was gone! for I knew that I belonged here,
abandoned and yet not, but one tiny dot
among all the others, all my sisters, brothers.

LITTLE LIGHT

for Susan Cataldo

To wake every morning to the
sound of my mother's voice
saying "C'mon, Susan, shower!"
So I undressed quickly, lay
breathless in bed. We lived safe
and sound in that building until
I was nine. Took showers in the
summer rain, long romantic walks
in my mind. Love was a song I heard
somewhere, someone, sometime,
over the radio, moon and croon.
Tonight, my face is night. Into it,
a white bird flies. I was 16 before I
ever realized, and when I woke up,
it was still night, so I crawled back
inside. You ask what's inside? In
side it, it's there's a light, little
light. It's death. It's life. And if you
take a picture, why you might even
find me, oh somewhere inside, and
I mean inside.

HOW WHY I WRITE

Studied "modern poetry" with some teachers
who they only got me angry to this very day,
which is probably why I think I've turned gay.
Man, do you put sunscreen on your penis? I do,
for it seems to me that the sun is after my penis
and wants to eat it or somesuch. Fell in love,
got married, must have been crazy, had kids,
one's on lap, other's ear, changed diapers,
changed jobs, wrote poems staring midnight
sun, got divorced, performs with a rockabilly
punk band called The Willies, gets drunk,
yeah I'm a bum. Crazy headaches that make me
shout filth, but otherwise, my pretty darklings,
Dad is yours. I have no regular "writing method"
unfortunately. Me, I'm primarily driven by
inspiration: i.e., the sun talks to me and I but
simply listen, nod my pointed head, and write
it down while Rome burns on. "Come put your
lips, love, upon these cheeks, and kissie me."
Tiny nips of tricky medications and, if all these
get them finally in place, the man gets to work.
I would be, I think, a better writer if only the
sun, wait, have I told you of that funny old sun?
for it seems to me

DAD

Yes, it often happens that
he's a man paint-splattered, he's Dad
Don't make that face, paint ducks, drink
hot milk. Just that something beneath his lip
& sleep, Mr. Milkman, for someday you will
Meanwhile, my horsie neighs, he's lonely
I show him my hands. See? Empty.
& there's Death riding come a riding
& good boys don't cry, he says, dying a dying
to climb a green hill, wake up, stand still
& hold me. Hold me. We count the silences
flying backwards. Some days take years
but let me just sit here. I'll just sit here, ok?

ROBERT FROST

Robert Frost wore a great gray suit and
he read to us in a deeply resonant voice,
for about an hour. The Y on 92nd St. had
a room set aside where we who bought
his book could go inside and have him,
Robert Frost, autograph it. Nervous, I
myself was just a nervous kid, the thought
of going to meet this great poet made me
so nervous, just to say, "Would you sign it
for me? My name is William." Ladies,
mostly ladies were on the line so when he,
Robert Frost saw me, he looked surprised.
"So you like poetry?" he, Robert Frost, he
asked me. "Your poetry, yes sir," I said.
"Studied you in school, your Mending Walls
and Stopping By Woods. Yes, and maybe
someday, if I study hard, I'll be a poet, too."
Robert Frost smiled, took my book, great
poet, and he quickly signed it, "To William,
with thanks for stopping by. Robert Frost."

THAT RADICAL

thought is a radical
that once I stumbled upon, gadzooks
complex, as complex, say, as Beauty
that one simply has to resolve every day

the subject/object thing, I mean. I
mean, you walk into a room and the room
is empty, so you think how very boring, the
room is empty. But the room is not really

empty, is it? I mean, you. You're in it, Sweets.
I stumbled upon this, in a way, in the 1960s
and Andy said, "Because it's not important."
and like Wow, that just blew my mind, because

in other words, I look around the world
and, as I do, is it my imagination or
are we, even as we stand here, simply disappearing
you, society, goodbye. And you, identity

Because what's really the answer to "Who am I
and why why am I here on this sinking island?"
and that how many things become invisible, unreal
which once were very and terribly real

and for why it is not, in fact, at all true. Truth
is how do you actually, in real time, do that?
For even as I talk and you stand and listen
at first, politely, and then to my dread I see you yawn

and you topple over, bang! Are you alive or dead?
Why, I simply have to wonder! All these thoughts like
dust, and so I am undone. I begin, at last, to
realize that, alas, without you, there is no beginning

and there is no middle and there is no end. The truth
is I'm not even born. I haven't even been born.

MICKEY AND THE MOOSE

I was about 3 years old in Wyoming and
on a porch and a moose came up to me
and just stared at me for a while. So I
said hello there Mister Moose and the
moose looked at me and went Moooz. I
sure got scared but then my Dad came
out on the porch and he saw the moose
and he waved his arms and he shouted
Shoo! So the Moose got scared and he
turned around and went away. My Dad
asked me if I was scared and I said Yes
so my Dad said you are a boy and boys
should not get scared but whenever you
do get scared you just go Shoo! So that's
what I do now whenever I get scared I
just wave my arms like I'm all crazy and
I just go Shoo! And for my 3rd birthday,
let me tell you where they both took me,
my parents took me to Disney's World,
what a great place! I remember going
up to Mickey and telling him I was three
years old. Mickey, he put one hand of his
around my shoulders and held up his other
hand up with three fingers. Then, my Mom
she snapped a picture. What a great picture!
I'm looking at it right now. Gee, it's just
me and Mickey. Hi, Mickey! That is the
one moment in my life I don't think I will
ever forget.

In addition to his eight books of poems, Bill Kushner

has worked as a playwright, actor, and directer at the

New York Theatre Ensemble and Theater Genesis in

New York. He has just finished *Good Gravy Marie*, a

new full-length play.

Made in the USA
Monee, IL
07 July 2026

56679121R00052